Curtio precipitato
et altri capricii (1638)

Recent Researches in Music

A-R Editions publishes seven series of critical editions, spanning the history of Western music, American music, and oral traditions.

Recent Researches in the Music of the Middle Ages and Early Renaissance
 Charles M. Atkinson, general editor

Recent Researches in the Music of the Renaissance
 James Haar, general editor

Recent Researches in the Music of the Baroque Era
 Steven Saunders, general editor

Recent Researches in the Music of the Classical Era
 Neal Zaslaw, general editor

Recent Researches in the Music of the Nineteenth and Early Twentieth Centuries
 Rufus Hallmark, general editor

Recent Researches in American Music
 John M. Graziano, general editor

Recent Researches in the Oral Traditions of Music
 Philip V. Bohlman, general editor

Each edition in *Recent Researches* is devoted to works by a single composer or to a single genre. The content is chosen for its high quality and historical importance and is edited according to the scholarly standards that govern the making of all reliable editions.

For information on establishing a standing order to any of our series, or for editorial guidelines on submitting proposals, please contact:

A-R Editions, Inc.
Middleton, Wisconsin

800 736-0070 (North American book orders)
608 836-9000 (phone)
608 831-8200 (fax)
http://www.areditions.com

RECENT RESEARCHES IN THE MUSIC OF THE BAROQUE ERA, 177

Tarquinio Merula

Curtio precipitato et altri capricii (1638)

Edited by Phoebe Jevtovic

A-R Editions, Inc.
Middleton, Wisconsin

A-R Editions, Inc., Middleton, Wisconsin
© 2012 by A-R Editions, Inc.

All rights reserved. No part of this book may be reproduced or transmitted in any form by any electronic or mechanical means (including photocopying, recording, or information storage and retrieval) without permission in writing from the publisher.

The purchase of this edition does not convey the right to perform it in public, nor to make a recording of it for any purpose. Such permission must be obtained in advance from the publisher.

A-R Editions is pleased to support scholars and performers in their use of *Recent Researches* material for study or performance. Please visit our website (www.areditions.com) to apply for permission to perform, record, or otherwise reuse the material in this publication.

Printed in the United States of America

ISBN 978-0-89579-732-2
ISSN 0484-0828

∞ The paper used in this publication meets the minimum requirements of the American National Standard for Information Sciences—Permanence of Paper for Printed Library Materials, ANSI Z39.48-1992.

Contents

Acknowledgments vi

Introduction vii
  Biography vii
  Merula's Vocal Music vii
  The Music of *Curtio precipitato* viii
  Notes on Performance ix
  Notes x

Texts and Translations xi

Plates xxiii

Curtio precipitato et altri capricii

  Dedication 3
  Dedicatory Sonnets 3
    1. Curtio, ove vai? 5
    2. Fiori, fiori, o quanti fiori 18
    3. Folle è ben che si crede 22
    4. Conza lavez e colder 23
    5. Sempre lieta, gioconda, e brillante 24
    6. Un pastorel nato non so 25
    7. Non mi chiedete, o fidi amici 26
    8. Quando gli uccelli porteranno i zoccoli 27
    9. Quand'io volsi l'altra sera 31
    10. Menti, lingua bugiarda 32
    11. Hor ch'è tempo di dormire 35
    12. Chi vuol ch'io m'innamori 40
    13. Un bambin che và alla scola 41
    14. El me tira nott'e dì 42
    15. Non ha 'l regno d'amor 42
    16. Sentirete una canzonetta 43

Critical Report 45
  Editorial Methods 45
  Critical Notes 46

Acknowledgments

I offer eternal gratitude to James Tyler for his mentorship throughout my graduate studies at the University of Southern California. The USC Early Music Ensemble offered not only vibrant, excellent performance experiences, but served as a workshop in historically-informed musicianship. My thanks also go to the ensemble La Monica, with whom I was able to explore many of the songs of this volume in performance. I am particularly grateful to Larry Rosenwald, Anne Desler, and Giulio Ongaro for their linguistic expertise, and their generosity in translating the song texts of this edition. Eric Smigel, Joyce Tyler, and Avi Stein were meticulous, kind, and supportive proofreaders. Lastly, the Art Monastery Project in Italy provided me with an invaluable artist residency which provided a writing desk, a stunning view, and my husband.

Introduction

Biography

Tarquinio Merula, born in Busseto in 1595,[1] was an innovative composer of keyboard, string, and vocal music, as well as a virtuoso organist, choirmaster, and violinist. His early musical training and experience took place in Cremona, but little else is known, as Merula himself was a bit secretive about his musical beginnings. While his first experience as a church organist was probably at San Bartolomeo in Cremona,[2] it is not clear whether he held that post officially or simply played there often; furthermore, in the preface to his *Il primo libro delle canzoni*,[3] he refers to his study of organ and composition, but does not name any teachers. In the same preface he downplays the existence of any possible rivals he might have had in Cremona, contending that he spent little time in the company of skilled organists.

A year after his first publication appeared, Merula accepted a three-year contract as organist at Santa Maria Incoronata in Lodi, and another that was offered to him when that term expired. However, a year into his second term he accepted a post as organist at a more prestigious musical establishment, the court of King Sigismund III in Warsaw, where he remained until early 1624. It is not known where he spent the next two years of his life, but from June through September of 1624 he managed to have three volumes of his music published in Venice: *Il primo libro de' madrigaletti*, *Il primo libro delle madrigali concertati*, and *Il primo libro de' motetti e sonate concertati*.[4]

His next appointment was as *maestro di cappella* for the Laudi della Madonna at the cathedral in Cremona, a post which, as the chapel's name suggests, required him to provide the music for a weekly Saturday evening service in celebration of the Litany of the Blessed Virgin. During his first year there he published *Satiro e Corisca*, a musical dialogue based on Guarini's *Il Pastor Fido*, and two years later his *Libro secondo de concerti spirituali* appeared.[5] In the preface to the latter publication, Merula refers to yet another post, organist at the Chiesa collegiata di Santa Agata, which he held in addition to his ongoing duties at Cremona Cathedral.

In 1631 Merula was offered and accepted a post in Bergamo as *maestro di cappella* of Santa Maria Maggiore. This position, his most important to date, had become vacant the previous year when the estimable Alessandro Grandi fell victim to the plague. Merula's tenure at Santa Maria Maggiore was brief but productive. During the two years of his residence in Bergamo, two new volumes of music appeared: *Il secondo libro delle canzoni* and *Madrigali et altre musiche concertate*.[6] Merula was unable to complete his three-year term at Santa Maria Maggiore, however. He was accused of indecent behavior towards some of the choristers in his charge and, faced with the threat of termination and the scandal of a criminal trial, resigned and returned to Cremona, where he resumed his employment at the Cappella della Laudi. Within two years, however, his salary having been reduced to what he considered an unacceptable level, he also resigned from the Cappella delle Laudi. His whereabouts between 1635 and 1638 are not known, but his musical activities certainly did not cease. This period of apparent unemployment saw the publication of *Pegaso opra musicale*,[7] a volume of sacred music, followed by *Canzoni overo sonate concertati per chiesa e camera*,[8] and *Curtio precipitato*.[9]

An opportunity to take up a position as *maestro di cappella* of the Duomo, adjacent to Santa Maria Maggiore, recalled Merula to Bergamo in 1638. Although it is completely understandable that he would wish to accept a position of such prestige, it is nonetheless surprising that he would do so, considering that it meant returning to the scene of his previous disgrace. And indeed, the old enmity soon rose to the surface again. In 1642 the ruling council of Santa Maria Maggiore forbade their musicians to perform under Merula's direction in the cathedral, and, whether for that reason or another, he abandoned his position at the Duomo.

Evidence of Merula's activities from 1642 to 1646 is scarce. It is known that he was one of four composers who set Giulio Strozzi's libretto for the opera *La finta savia*, which was performed in Venice in 1643; but it is not until August of 1646 that Merula's actual whereabouts are known. At that time he returned to his native Cremona, where he resumed his duties as *maestro di cappella* and organist of the Cappella delle Laudi, as well as organist of the cathedral. During the last two decades of his life, Merula published only two more volumes: *Il quarto libro da suonare* followed a year later by his final opus, *Il terzo libro delli salmi et messa concertati*.[10] Although his compositional output had slowed considerably, he continued to perform his various duties at the Cremona Cathedral until his death on 10 December 1665.

Merula's Vocal Music

Like his contemporaries, Merula wrote sacred and secular vocal music in the genres of the motet, madrigal, canzonetta, and aria. At that time, vocal music displayed features of both sixteenth-century polyphony and the new monodic style of solo song with basso continuo. Indeed, it was not uncommon for the two styles to be found side by side within the same piece, whether sacred or secular. The concerted madrigal, for example, was beginning to exhibit more virtuosic solo writing than it had in the sixteenth century, when equal-voiced polyphony was the rule.

Although Merula is known largely for the inventiveness of his instrumental compositions (particularly those for organ and violin), his first publication, *Il primo libro delle canzoni,* shows characteristics that later would distinguish his vocal compositions. It contains artful chromaticism and ground bass (*basso ostinato*) patterns. His use of these repeated bass patterns was a thread that he wove into every genre in which he wrote; even his *Messa concertata a tre* (1640) is based on the Ruggiero pattern, making it the only mass on a ground bass published theretofore. One of the most striking examples of Merula's use of a ground bass appears in his *Madrigali et altre musiche concertante*: the aria "Su la cetra amorosa" is composed over an ingeniously-wrought chaconne that deftly modulates twelve times, traveling through six different key centers.

Merula and his older contemporary Claudio Monteverdi appear to have influenced each other. While Monteverdi certainly exerted the greatest influence he was not necessarily always the innovator. Merula's setting of "Beatus vir" from *Pegaso musicale,* for example, employs the Romanesca two years earlier than Monteverdi's published ground-bass setting of the same text in *Selva morale e spirituale* (1640). *Selva morale* contains another text set by both composers, "Chi vuol ch'io m'innamori," which had already been published in Merula's *Curtio precipitato* (1638). Monteverdi may, as was his wont, have composed the pieces years before their publication, but it is possible that Merula had precedence. Monteverdi's imprint upon Merula and other fellow composers can be seen in numerous tributes and parodies such as "Curtio, ove vai?" from *Curtio precipitato.* As Merula's only surviving collection devoted exclusively to solo songs, *Curtio precipitato* is also the definitive work in any discussion of Merula's vocal compositional style.

The Music of *Curtio precipitato*

As the title *Curtio precipitato et altri capricii* suggests, most of the volume consists of frivolous, lighthearted songs, often with a satirical twist. "Fiori, fiori, o quanti fiori," for example, is particularly easygoing, consisting mainly of a sequence of lazily-descending arpeggios. Combined with the fatuousness of its text, it seems to poke fun at the simple melodies that had begun to characterize solo arias. Silke Leopold points to the subtle metrical displacements in this song as a spoof of the contemporary craze for repetitive rhythmic structures in Italian song.[11] Merula's penchant for mocking turns a corner in the song "Quando gli uccelli," which appears at first to be a mere vehicle for fantastic, surreal, ridiculous *sdrucciolo* rhymes (wherein the syllabic emphasis falls on the antepenultimate). The declamatory setting over sustained notes in the bass spoofs the by then old-fashioned, heroic style, which is distorted here both by the *sdrucciolo* endings and the ridiculous verbiage. Nearly every phrase accelerates to an impossible punch line of sorts, but each verse also concludes with a sad revelation of underlying suffering, set to large ascending leaps and longer note values.

The first song in the volume, "Curtio, ove vai?," deserves special mention as a musical satire. Music historians Denis Arnold[12] and Silke Leopold[13] have each speculated on the relationship between this piece and Monteverdi's *Combattimento di Tancredi e Clorinda*. Both works are centered upon heroes of mythic proportions: Monteverdi's Tancredi and Clorinda, characters from Tasso's epic poem, *Gerusalemme Liberata,* and Merula's hero, Marcus Curtius, a figure of Roman popular legend. Each offers a musical depiction of galloping steeds. Monteverdi's "motto del cavallo" is scored for two violins, viola, and continuo and underscores several pages of narrative. Although Merula's elaborately titled "sinfonia ad imitatione d'un Cavallo" is simply a three-measure gesture in the bass line, he lists the section separately in the table of contents. While one might speculate that Merula originally wrote string parts for *Curtio* that either were not published or have since been lost, it is more likely that the pitifully anticlimactic "sinfonia ad imitatione d'un Cavallo" was intended as part of the joke. Merula, in the dedication of the volume, had already played upon the pun of Marco Curtio's name meaning "short," and one would be hard-pressed to find a sinfonia shorter than this one. Thus, while the pieces are musically similar, the text of "Curtio, ove vai?" presents a rather cynical parody of the type of heroic idealism found in Monteverdi's *Combattimento*.

For context, we must be familiar with the story of our volume's titular hero. First-century historian Titus Livius recounted the story of Marcus Curtius thusly: in 362 BC, a chasm opened up in the middle of the Roman Forum leading down toward Hades. The people began to try to close it, making ceremonial offerings, but the abyss was unaffected. When the people asked the soothsayers what to do, they answered that the chasm would only be closed by putting into it "the most precious thing of all." The Romans then tried filling it with many different precious offerings, but the chasm still did not close. Then a young Roman cavalier named Marcus Curtius had an inspiration: the most precious thing Rome could offer had to be the strength and courage of a Roman soldier. So, wearing all of his weapons, and riding the finest warhorse, he threw himself into the abyss as a sacrifice. The hole immediately closed behind him, and the people were freed from its menace. It was said that Marcus Curtius did not die, but rather went directly to the underworld, intact in his youth and valor.[14] A later Renaissance interpretation would hold that he joined the damned in Hell—an even greater sacrifice.[15]

At first glance, this seems the perfect subject for a volume of songs financed by and dedicated to a military man (Giovanni Battista Barbo). However, one wonders how Merula got away with such deep irreverence in his treatment of Curtio's heroic act, as he seems to imply ridicule of his own patron's profession. Indeed, Merula's music mocks the heroic soldier at every turn. Aside from the stream of cynical verbal putdowns, the song is full of musical puns: for example, a sprightly Ruggiero bass pattern appears in the continuo part at the mention in the text of the character Ruggiero (a descendant of Hector, another epic hero). The Ruggiero is followed by an iteration of the brief sinfonia, which seems more absurd at each appearance. In setting the text "Ch'io non vi niego questo, ma non sarebbe morto così presto" (Though I do not deny that he would have died, he would not have died so soon), Merula employs a sarcastic lament bass pattern that is musically sweet, but betrayed by the words, which are essentially another tasteless joke about the brevity of Curtio's life. Silke Leopold points out that this cynical take on the heroic tale might itself be a sort of tribute to Barbo, who as the Cremonese commander would have had little incentive to risk his life for the Spanish powers currently in control of the territory.[16]

Musically, the aria is full of incredibly demanding passagework, and requires a singer with a rather wide vocal range (C to e♭'). However, as there was not yet a standardized frequency for pitches, transposition is a perfectly acceptable performance solution. See the following section regarding performance notes for more on this topic.

Although the phrase *altri capricii* in the title leads one to believe that the entire volume consists of lighthearted songs, there are a few rather serious and poignant pieces that stand out as exceptions. The most stunning of these is "Hor ch'è tempo di dormire," with its mesmerizing two-note repeated bass. The simple, rocking alternation of a semitone underscores and contradicts the haunting and lyrical lullaby sung by the Virgin Mary. "Folle è ben che si crede" is deceptively simple, with its melody consisting mostly of scalar motion. But it is lovely in its faithful sentiment accentuated by chains of suspensions and intensified by an unexpected modal shift from C to B♭ in the middle of the song.

Merula also makes use of popular traditions in this volume. The carnival song "Conza lavez e colder" is written in a northern mountain dialect, recalling the cries of a street vendor. As is typical for this genre, the text is rife with double meanings, describing an itinerant tinsmith who may be handling far more than the local pots and pans.[17] The last song in the volume, "Sentirete una canzonetta," is based on the popular Girometta melody (a Northern Italian dance tune). This melody forms the basis of many other Italian pieces of the time, including Frescobaldi's "cappricio sopra la Girolmeta" from *Fiori musicali*.[18] It stands out as the only piece in the volume with a melodic instrumental ritornello, and uses a highly unusual continuo notation with two bass lines. One of the bass lines is a simple drone on a low C, and the other an ostinato repeating the fifth and octave, probably an imitation of popular drone instruments such as the hurdy-gurdy or *zampogna* (bagpipe). The last verse of this last song ends in humorous hyperbole: "I have come to the end," the speaker says, referring to his life; although Merula, of course, is referring to his *Curtio*.

Notes on Performance

Any musician approaching this repertoire must become acquainted with Giulio Caccini's monument to stylish singing, *Le nuove musiche* (Firenze, 1602).[19] In it, Caccini advocates for an emotionally affective approach to a solo vocal line, emphasizing clarity and ease of expression of the text. The introduction to the volume explains and recommends ornaments such as the trillo (a percussive glottal re-striking of one note), gruppo (something like our modern conception of a trill followed by a turn), and other graces designed to create an emotional response in the listener. Merula generally leaves ornamentation to the discretion of the singer, but in measures 206–7 and 301–2 of "Curtio, ove vai?" we find instances of a string of repeated sixteenth notes within a long melisma. Above each, Merula makes the indication of "t.," confirming that those passages must be treated as the above-mentioned trillo. By no means should those notes be elided, but rather a fluttering, almost giggling approach is needed. For guidance on tempo, mensural notation, and rhythmic conversion relationships, George Houle's *Meter in Music* is an inspiring source of information that emphasizes an understanding of the tactus (the underlying beat) rather than a reliance on tempo markings.[20] As for instrumentation, a solo voice and at least one chordal instrument is the minimum, but there is much room for variety even in this configuration. Players who are trained to realize basso continuo lines have great freedom to illustrate the text (by their voicing and articulation) employing a creativity and drama equal to the singer's.[21]

Notes

1. Merula was baptized in Busseto on 25 November 1595, so we may assume he was born no more than a few weeks prior to that date; see Joachim Steinheuer, *Chamäleon und Salamander: Neue Wege der Textvertonung bei Tarquinio Merula* (New York: Bärenreiter, 1999), 16. Many sources, including the most recent edition of the *New Grove Dictionary of Music and Musicians*, incorrectly cite Merula's birthplace as Cremona, placing the date within 1594–95, based on his confirmation date (23 April 1607); cf. *Grove Music Online*, Oxford Music Online (http://www.oxfordmusiconline.com), s.v. "Merula, Tarquinio," by Stephen Bonta (accessed 12 December 2011).

2. Christopher Wilkinson cites a contemporary reference to Merula as a master organist and contrapuntist who had been organist at San Bartolomeo for many years. These years would have been, by necessity, before his appointment in Lodi in 1616. See Wilkinson, "The Sacred Music of Tarquinio Merula" (Ph.D. diss., Rutgers University, 1978), 71 n. 19.

3. *Il primo libro delle canzoni, a 4* (Venice, 1615); Répertoire International des Sources Musicales (hereafter RISM), *Einzeldrucke vor 1800*, ser. A/I (Kassel: Bärenreiter, 1971–81), M 2352.

4. *Il primo libro de' madrigaletti a tre voci . . . opera quarta* (Venice, 1624), RISM A/I, M 2344; *Il primo libro delle madrigali concertati a quattro, cinque, sei, sette & otto voci con il suo basso continuo . . . opera quinta* (Venice, 1624), RISM A/I, M 2345; and *Il primo libro de' motetti e sonate concertati . . . opera sei* (Venice, 1624), RISM A/I, M 2338.

5. *Satiro e Corisca dialogo musicale* (Venice, 1626), RISM A/I, M 2347; *Libro secondo de concerti spirituali con alcune sonate* (Venice, 1628), RISM A/I, M 2339.

6. *Il secondo libro delle canzoni da suonare à tre* (Venice, ca. 1631–33), RISM A/I, M 2354; *Madrigali et altre musiche concertate* (Venice, 1633), RISM A/I, M 2348.

7. *Pegaso opra musicale l'undecima que s'adono salmi, motetti, suonate, e letaniae della B. V.* (Venice, ca. 1635–37), RISM A/I, M 2341.

8. *Canzoni overo sonate concertati per chiesa e camera a due et a tre . . . libro terzo* (Venice, 1637), RISM A/I, M 2353. This title represents the first time that the terms *sonata* and *canzona* are used synonymously; see Wilkinson, "Sacred Music," 85.

9. *Curtio precipitato et altri capricii, libro secondo* (Venice, 1638), RISM A/I, M 2351.

10. *Il quarto libro delle canzoni da suonare* (Venice, 1651), RISM A/I, M 2356; *Il terzo libro delle salmi et messa concertati a tre et a quattro . . . opera XVIII* (Venice, 1652), RISM A/I, M 2343.

11. Silke Leopold, *Al modo d'Orfeo: Dichtung und Musik im italienischen Sologesang des frühen 17. Jahrhunderts* (Laaber: Laaber-Verlag, 1995), 112–13.

12. Arnold makes a brief reference to the works' similarities in "Monteverdi: Some Colleagues and Pupils," in *The New Monteverdi Companion,* ed. Denis Arnold and Nigel Fortune (London: Faber and Faber, 1985), 120.

13. Silke Leopold addresses the relationship in depth in "Curtio Precipitato–Claudio Parodiato," in *The Well Enchanting Skill: Music, Poetry, and Drama in the Culture of the Renaissance: Essays in Honour of F. W. Sternfeld,* ed. John Caldwell, Edward Olleson, and Susan Wollenberg (Oxford: Clarendon Press, 1990), 65–76.

14. For the sources of this legend, see *A Topographical Dictionary of Ancient Rome,* by Samuel Ball Platner, completed and revised by Thomas Ashby (London: Oxford University Press, 1929), s.v. "Lacus Curtius."

15. For more on later interpretations of the legend, see Marc Laureys, "Civic Self-Offering: Some Renaissance Representations of Marcus Curtius," in *Recreating Ancient History: Episodes from the Greek and Roman Past in the Arts and Literature of the Early Modern Period,* ed. Karl. A. Enenkel, Jan L. de Jong, and Jeanine de Landtsheer (Leiden: Brill, 2001), 147–66.

16. Leopold, "Curtio Precipitato," 69.

17. For more on the carnival song tradition, see Bonnie J. Blackburn, "Two 'Carnival Songs' Unmasked: A Commentary on MS Florence Magl. XIX. 121," *Musica Disciplina* 35 (1981): 121–78.

18. For more on the Girometta, see Warren Kirkendale, "Franceschina, Girometta, and their Companions in a Madrigal 'a diversi linguaggi' by Luca Marenzio and Orazio Vecchi," *Acta Musicologica* 44 (1972): 181–235.

19. A modern edition is available in Giulio Caccini, *Le nouve musiche,* ed. H. Wiley Hitchcock, Recent Researches in the Music of the Baroque Era, vol. 9, 2nd ed. (Middleton, Wis.: A-R Editions, 2009).

20. George Houle, *Meter in Music, 1600–1800: Performance, Perception, and Notation* (Bloomington: Indiana University Press, 1987).

21. For more on appropriate performance practice see Robert Donington, *The Interpretation of Early Music,* new rev. ed. (New York: Norton, 1992), and *A Performer's Guide to Seventeenth-Century Music,* ed. Stewart Carter (New York: Schirmer, 1997).

Texts and Translations

The text has been taken intact from the original print, with the following modifications: Seventeenth-century word forms have been retained where appropriate ("gratiosa" for "graziosa," for example), but inconsistencies in the orthography and punctuation have been modernized; for example, the use of *j* for *i*, inconsistent observation of double consonants, etc. Abbreviations have been tacitly expanded. The layout of the verses follows the versification suggested by the original text, and does not always reflect the layout in the underlaid stanzas of the print, in which lines are often broken into shorter segments to reflect internal rhymes. Translations for nos. 3, 6, 9, and 11 were provided by Lawrence Rosenwald, no. 4 by Giulio Ongaro, and Anne Desler provided the remainder.

1. Curtio, ove vai?

Curtio, ove vai?
   Non far questa pazzia.
   Fermati col malan che Dio ti dia!
   Che se tu salti te ne pentirai.
   A che pensando stai
   circa al gettarti a basso?
   Tu ti puoi scapriciare,
   ma quanto al ritornare,
   fratello mio, sarà un difficil passo.
   Non ti dar il tracollo!
   Ferma, ch'in fede mia ti rompi il collo.
O quai capricci strani
   ti saltan musa a dosso!
   Perché ti prendi gl'impacci del rosso
   con voler raddrizzar le gambe ai cani?
   Questi schiamazzi vani
   hor non servano a niente,
   che quel matto cornuto
   in som'è risoluto
   saltando voler dar gusto a la gente
   non gl'haver compassione
   anzi se vol cader dagli un urtone.
Da capo a piedi armato
   a guisa d'un Ruggiero
   con gale e con penacchi in su 'l destriero
   s'è nell'alta voragine gettato.
   Povero disgratiato,
   ch'humor ti venne in testa?
   Io la ragione spesso
   a pensar mi son messo,
   che te c'indusse, e sol vi trovo questa:
   convien che l'habbi fatto
   non per altro se non perch'eri un matto.

Curtio, where are you going?
   Do not do such a foolish thing.
   Stop, or God may give you an illness!
   For if you jump you will be sorry for it.
   What are you thinking,
   throwing yourself into the depth?
   You can indulge your whim,
   but when it comes to returning,
   my brother, that will be a difficult step.
   Do not throw yourself down!
   Stop, for, by my faith, you will break your neck.
Oh, what strange whims
   jump around in your head!
   Why bring the encumbrance of your roan
   on your mission to straighten out the dogs' legs?
   These vain reprimands
   will not serve any purpose now,
   since that mad dimwit
   has certainly resolved
   to amuse the indifferent people by jumping
   even though they would push him in,
   since he is so keen on it.
Armed from head to foot,
   looking like Ruggiero,
   in regalia and with plumes on his war horse,
   he has thrown himself into the deep gulf.
   Poor wretch,
   what fancy came into your head?
   I have often thought very hard
   to find a reason for which you jumped,
   and this is the only one I could come up with:
   it must be that you did it
   only because you were a lunatic.

Forse alcuno dirami	Some may say
a la Patria smarita	that for his homeland in distress
volle sacrificar la propria vita,	he wanted to sacrifice his own life,
facendo attione degna d'epigrammi.	doing deeds worthy of epigrams.
Hor questo stupir fammi	I however, am wondering:
perché gl'homini scaltri	how can intelligent men,
e quelli ch'hann giuditio,	judicious people
veduto il precipitio,	witness such an act,
stanno a vedere e fanno saltar gl'altri,	just standing there, allowing another to jump,
e in passi così brutti	and, in such ugly situations,
usano a dar la precedenza a tutti.	make others go first?
S'io fossi stato all'hora,	If I had been there,
vi dico il mio pensiero:	I will tell you what I would have done:
non gl'havrei fatto a fè da cavagliero,	I would not at all have acted gallantly,
e fosse andato pur Roma in mal'hora.	even were a misfortune to have befallen Rome.
So ch'il medesmo ancora	I know that someone else
fatto alcun altro havria,	would still have done the same,
e prima di cadere	and beforehand
saria stato a vedere	it would have been plain to see
come quel capitombo lo riusciva	how that headlong fall was going to turn out,
e d'imitarlo invece	so instead of imitating him
havrebbe riso poi di chi lo fece.	I would have laughed at him who jumped.
Che circa a quella gloria	For that kind of glory
dov'il lor fondamento	that these airheads
sanno questi pallon gonfii di vento,	consider to be profound,
com'esser nominati in un istoria,	like being mentioned in a story,
è una certa boria	is just a certain vainglory
da darle la coperta,	to give them comfort;
e un ente immaginario	it is the illusory product
di cervel temerario,	of a reckless brain;
ne d'esser crompo a tanto prezzo merta	Being spoken of does not merit the price
morire. O sfortunato,	of death. O misfortunate man,
perché? Per esser poscia nominato!	why? In order to be mentioned afterwards!
Ditemi in cortesia,	Be so kind as to tell me—
se mentre uno sta in Roma,	If while someone is in Rome
un'altro in India con honor lo noma,	someone else in India honors him,
non saprei che gusto ei n'haveria?	what pleasure could he derive from it?
Nessuno, in fede mia!	None, by my faith!
Che vengavi il mal anno.	May misfortune befall you
Ch'occorron tante glose,	When so many glosses occur,
quest'anime famose,	these famous minds,
che gusto ponno haver se non lo sanno?	what pleasure could they gain if they do not know about it?
Poich'a gl'homini morti,	After all, there is no messenger
non gl'è proccacio che gl'avisi porti.	who takes news to the dead.
Curtio aquistossi lode	Curtio acquired praise
d'animo bravo e forte,	for being a courageous and strong soul
poiche con quel saltar si die la morte.	after he killed himself with that jump.
Ma mentre non lo sa che cosa gode.	But meanwhile, he does not know what he enjoys.
E voi, persone sode,	And you, reasonable people,
hor non mi state a dire	Do not tell me
che tanto poco dopo	that he would,
gli fora stato d'uopo	soon afterwards,
al suo marcio dispetto al fin morire.	have had to die anyway.
Ch'io non vi niego questo,	Though I do not deny that he would have died,
ma non sarebbe morto così presto.	he would not have died so soon.
Hor voi ch'havete inteso	Now, all of you who have heard about
la pazzia di costui:	the folly of that man:
ecci alcun che sia pazzo al par di lui?	is there among you anyone who is that crazy?
Ditemi pur fra voi chi sarà quello	Tell me straightaway who among you
di si poco cervello	could have so little brain

che per lasciar che dire	that, just to be mentioned
a la plebe ignorante	by ignorant people,
si contenta morire.	would be happy to die?
Vadassi ad impicar pur chi n'hà voglia,	May whoever feels like it go to hang himself,
che morirà giocondo	for he will die a happy man
e darà dopo se che dire al mondo.	giving the world something to talk about.

Comment. Second stanza, fourth line, "to straighten out the dog's legs," i.e., to do something impossible.

2. Fiori, fiori, o quanti fiori

Prima parte

Fiori, fiori, o quanti fiori	Flowers, flowers, oh, how many flowers
qui ne spuntano l'herbette!	are sprouting here on the grass!
Su, su, ninfe amorosette	Come, come, little amorous nymphs,
qui drizzate i pie volanti.	Direct your light feet to this place.
corri Lilla, corri Clori,	Come running, Lilla, come running, Clori,
fiori, fiori, o quanti fiori!	flowers, flowers, oh, how many flowers!
Coglietene cento,	Pick a hundred,
coglietene mille,	pick a thousand of them,
dell'aure tranquille	Smelling the fragrances
del placido vento	of the tranquil breezes
sentire gl'odori:	of the placid wind:
o quanti, o quanti fiori!	oh, how many flowers!

Seconda parte

Ecco qui poggio reale	See here the royal hill
a cui sempre il sol riluce	on which the sun always shines,
che d'altrond'i raggi e luce	for from nowhere does it receive
non riceve ad altri eguale	equal rays and light
che da proprii suoi splendori:	as from its own splendors:
fiori, fiori, o quanti fiori!	flowers, flowers, oh, how many flowers!
Venite al prato	Come to the meadow,
venite al bosco	come to the forest,
che dentr'al più fosco	for in the darkest part inside
un giglio ho trovato	I have found a lily
di mille colori:	of a thousand colors:
o quanti, o quanti fiori!	oh, how many, how many flowers!

Terza parte

Questo candido narciso	This snow-white narcissus
ch'io ti dono e questa rosa,	that I give you and this rose,
Lilla mia vaga amorosa,	my pretty and lovely Lilla,
mi rasembra il tuo bel viso,	seems to me to resemble your beautiful face,
esca dolce a nostri ardori:	sweet tinder for our passion:
fiori, fiori, o quanti fiori!	flowers, flowers, oh, how many flowers.
Da varie foglie	From various flowers
cogliete, intrecciate	gather, weave
ghirlande odorate,	fragrant garlands;
facciate le voglie	do the bidding
di questi tesori:	of these treasures:
o quanti, o quanti fiori!	oh, how many flowers!

Quarta parte

Mira, mira le viole	Look, see the violets,
che biancheggiano gli acanti	the acanthus are blooming white,
e rossegian gl'amaranti.	and the amaranths are blushing.
N'ha la man quanti ne vole,	The hand can find as many as it wants,
ma son questi de minori:	but they are among the least:
fiori, fiori, o quanti fiori!	flowers, flowers, oh, how many flowers!
O vedi tu come	Oh, look how
quest'altro più grande	this other, larger flower

superbo ne spande
le candide chiome,
quest'altro qui fuori:
o quanti, o quanti fiori!

haughtily spreads
her fair hair,
this other one here outside:
oh, how many, how many flowers!

3. *Folle è ben che si crede*

Folle è ben che si crede
   che per dolce lusinghe amorose
   o per fiere minaccie sdegnose
   dal bel idolo mio ritraga il piede.
   Cangi pur suo pensiero
   ch'il mio cor prigioniero
   spera che goda la libertà.
   Dica chi vuole, dica chi sa.

Altri per gelosia
   spiri pur empie fiamme dal seno
   versi pure Megera il veneno
   perché rompi al mio ben la fede mia.
   Morte il viver mi toglia
   mai sia ver che si scioglia
   quel caro laccio che preso m'ha.
   Dica chi vuole, dica chi sa.

Ben havrò tempo, e loco
   da sfogar l'amorose mie pene
   da temprar de l'amato mio bene
   e de l'arso mio cor, l'occulto foco,
   e tra l'ombre, e gli orrori
   de notturni splendori
   il mio ben furto s'asconderà.
   Dica chi vuole, dica chi sa.

Mad is the man who thinks
   that for sweet and amorous flattery,
   or proud and haughty threats,
   I would turn my steps away from my beautiful idol.
   Let him give up his belief
   that my imprisoned heart
   hopes to enjoy liberty.
   Let those speak who wish; let those speak who know.

Let others, out of jealousy,
   breathe foul flames from their hearts;
   let the Fury Megaera pour forth her venom
   to make me break my oath to my beloved.
   Death may snatch my life away,
   but never will it loosen
   this precious bond that has possessed me.
   Let those speak who wish; let those speak who know.

Soon I will have both time and place
   to vent my amorous pangs,
   to tune the secret fire
   of my beloved and of my flame-scarred heart;
   And among the shadows and terrors
   of nocturnal splendors,
   my beloved will be hiding secretly.
   Let those speak who wish; let those speak who know.

Pio di Savoia

Comment. The attribution is from *Bibliografia della musica italiana vocale profana pubblicata dal 1500 al 1700,* ed. Emil Vogel et al., 3 vols. (Pomezia: Staderini, [1977]), 2:1130.

4. *Conza lavez e colder*

O, conza lavez e colder e padèl
   chiavidur e sidèl lum cazzù candire,
   l'è chi 'l Parolot ch'è vegnù da Lugan,
   sù madón e tosan paregie i vos cotà
   conza caz, è cazzù, lum, padèl e stagna.

I' ho bon stagnado bona lima martel
   mantisit tinivel, e cient'olter meste
   se ghiss ou quai vas che fus rot, ò fes dan,
   non ve ste met affan, laghe ved portè scia
   conza caz, è cazzù, lum, padèl e stagna.

Affeda ch'aù sciur se völi ch'aù lavora
   ch'in mane de mez'hora vuoi faù stravede
   e si no v' content'à reson, e mesura
   vuoi perd la facchiura, el vos dagn' vuoi refa
   conza caz, è cazzù, lum, padèl e stagna.

Per cünt del mercà dan' vu la sentenza
   ch'au sciur inconsienza de sta al vos parè
   e s' n'hissou quatrin cosi in pront, ve promet
   de sav' anch'asper, sin che mi torno à passà
   conza caz, è cazzù, lum, padèl e stagna.

Here is the fellow who fixes pots and pans, locks, lamps, etc., here is Parolot, who has come from Lugano, come on ladies and boys, get your stuff ready! Down here I fix lamps, frying pans, and tins.

I have good tin, file, and hammer, [. . .] and I do a hundred other things. If there is some vase that is broken, or was damaged, do not worry, just bring it here. I fix . . .

You must come out if you want me to work, because in half an hour I will amaze you, and if you are not satisfied, I will lose my profit and give you back your money. I fix . . .

Because of this transaction, I want you to know that I am ready to serve you, and if you do not have your money ready, I promise I will wait, until the next time I come around. I fix . . .

Fronte st'occasion tant che son paregia
    che san' consorà da rial coldire
    e si non' do gust con si bella destrezza
    de fau per dolcezza romagn'incanta
    cacciem pur i sù forch', e mandem à inpica.

If all of this doesn't convince you, and you still do not want my services, the praises of which are sung far and wide, may I be taken to the gallows and condemned.

5. *Sempre lieta, gioconda, e brillante*

Sempre lieta, gioconda, e brillante,
    leggiadretta, gentile, e vezzosa,
    tutta viva, compita, e galante
    è la bella Dorina amorosa.
    Non è dama la più gratiosa,
    non è ninfa la più garbatina
    de la cara mia amata Dorina.
Se la ride, o la balla o canta,
    se la scherza, la guarda o lavora,
    la rapisce, la lega, l'incanta,
    la ferisce, l'accend'e innamora;
    ogn'un l'ama, la serva, e l'adora,
    ch'ella è troppo gustosa, e carina,
    la mia cara, amorosa Dorina.
Mai si turba, si sdegna, o s'adira,
    mai si mostra ritrosa, o rubella;
    anzi ascolta, gradisse, e rimira,
    compatisce, e cortese favella.
    Quanto è vaga, mirabile, e bella!
    Tanto è dolce gustosa mamina
    la mia cara diletta Dorina.
Gioia, gusto, piacer, e diletto,
    gaudio, pace, dolcezza, e contento
    spira e porge quel viso, e quel petto,
    quel leggiadro e gentil portamento.
    Ahi ch'al cielo rapire mi sento,
    quando miro, e vagheggio vicina
    la mia cara adorata Dorina!

Always happy, cheerful, and radiant,
    light-hearted, sweet-tempered, and pretty,
    all lively, well-bred, and gracious
    is the lovely, beautiful Dorina.
    There is no woman more graceful,
    there is no nymph more well-bred
    than my dear beloved Dorina.
Whether she laughs, dances or sings,
    whether teasing, gazing or working,
    she ravishes, she binds, she enchants,
    she wounds, she enflames, and enamors;
    everyone loves her, serves her, and adores her,
    for she is just too pleasant and darling,
    my dear beloved Dorina.
Never does she get upset, scornful, or angry,
    she never appears headstrong or defiant,
    instead she listens, is welcoming, and considerate,
    shows sympathy, and talks affably.
    How lovely, admirable, and beautiful she is!
    She is such a sweet pleasant little lady,
    my dear cherished Dorina.
Joy, pleasure, happiness, and delight,
    gladness, peace, sweetness, and contentment
    emanate from her face and her breast
    and her light-hearted and gentle bearing.
    Ah, I feel that I am carried away to heaven,
    when I gaze with delight and behold close to me
    my dear adored Dorina!

6. *Un pastorel nato non so*

Un pastorel nato non so,
    se di ninfa o di fera,
    crudo ma bel, quant'esser puo.
    Una beltà severa,
    fa impacir, fa impacir le donne a schiera
    fa stupire, fa languire, fa morir.
Belva non è ch'al lo suo stral
    schermir possa, o fuggire
    ne pari a se braccio mortal
    si vidde mai colpire
    ma d'amar, ma d'amar non vuol sentire,
    sono i canti, sono i pianti sparsi in van.
Cupido al fin quel grand'arcier
    trionfante de cori
    al cui divin alto poter
    cedon gli eccelsi chori
    affrenar, affrenar penso i furori
    di si altiere, di si fiero, spiritel.
Ma vinto ancor restò non men
    l'angiolin faretrato
    e di tremor sparso, e ripien
    gridò mercè prostrato,

There is this little shepherd, born maybe
    of a nymph, maybe of a beast,
    as harsh—and as handsome—as he can be.
    His unbending beauty
    drives the ladies crazy, crowds of them,
    he is stunning—he makes them languish and die.
There is no beast that can be shielded
    from his dart, or escape it,
    nor did any mortal arm
    ever strike the way he does.
    But he does not want to hear of love,
    and songs and laments are uttered in vain.
Finally Cupid, that great archer,
    victorious in all hearts,
    to whose lofty, divine power
    even the heavenly choirs yield,
    decided to rein in the rages
    of so bold and proud a sprite.
But the sharpshooting angel
    was also conquered,
    and, all covered with fear,
    he prostrate called out, "have pity!"

el pastor, el pastor vago, e spietato
d'arco e strali, sin del'ali lo spogliò.
Hor chi potrà già mai spiegar
  tal beltà si proterva,
  s'amor non ha per contrastar
  arma che più le serva?
  fugg'ogn'alm, fugg'ogn'alma come cerva
  ch'è s'è gionta, ch'è s'è punta guai a fe.

7. *Non mi chiedete, o fidi amici*

Non mi chiedete, o fidi amici,
  non ricercate o cari amanti
  perch'io tragga i di infelici
  in continui amari pianti
  ed in languidi sospir,
  che non lo posso dir.
Dama ch'adoro ha sparso il crine
  nel laberinto del mio core,
  le cui luci peregrine
  al sol furan lo splendore.
  Mi tormenta e fa languir
  e non gliel posso dir.
Deh, se puo mai sentir conforto!
  Ignudo spirto io prego almeno
  che dopo ch'io sarò morto
  mi fia tratto il cor dal seno,
  ch'ivi ogn'un potra scoprir
  ciò ch'hor non posso dir.
La bella imago, el gentil nome,
  dolce cagion de la mia morte
  qui vedransi al hor, e come
  fe tacermi invida sorte
  e forzommi al fin morir
  per non poter lo dir.

8. *Quando gli uccelli porteranno i zoccoli*

Prima parte

Quando gli uccelli porteranno i zoccoli
  e su per l'aria voleran gli buffoli,
  le rose e i gigli produrranno broccoli
  e le ranochie soneranno i zuffoli,
  il dì de morti sarà senza moccoli,
  nera la neve e blanche le tartuffoli,
  i ricchi zaperanno la cicoria
  prima che voi m'usciate di memoria.
Quando li muti canteranno favole
  e gli Tedeschi non sapran più bevere,
  li sorci piglieran le gatte gnavole
  e fuggiranno i cani da le lievere,
  quando sarà coperto il ciel di tavole,
  amaro sarà il zuccaro e dolce i pevere,
  il mar di piante, i monti d'acqua carichi:

  allora finiranno i miei rammarichi.

Seconda parte

Quando li grilli giocherann di scrimia
  e su le corde balleranno gl'asini,
  i cacciatori diverrann la simia
  e le cipolle produranno i pampani,

And the shepherd, charming and ruthless,
  stripped him of bow, arrow, and wings.
Who can ever deal with
  so impudent a beauty,
  if Love himself has no useful weapons
  for rebuking him?
  Let every soul flee like a doe—
  for if it is caught, if it is hit, there will be certain woe.

Do not ask me, o faithful friends,
  do not inquire, o dear lovers,
  why I spend my unhappy days
  in continuous bitter tears
  and in languid sighs,
  for I cannot tell you.
The Lady I adore has cast her hair
  into the labyrinth of my heart;
  her noble eyes
  steal the splendor of the sun.
  She torments me and makes me languish
  and I cannot tell her.
Ah, will I ever find comfort!
  I pray that at least after my death
  when I am a naked spirit,
  my heart be torn from my chest,
  so that then everyone will see
  that which now I cannot tell.
The beautiful face, the gentle name,
  sweet reasons for my death
  will then be seen here on my heart,
  and also how envious destiny made me silent
  and in the end forced me to die
  so I would not be able to tell.

The birds will wear galoshes
  and the buffalo fly through the air,
  roses and lilies will grow broccoli
  and the frogs play pipes,
  the day of the dead will be without candles,
  the snow black and the truffles white,
  the rich go digging for chicory
  before you will leave my memory.
When the mutes recite stories,
  and Germans don't know how to drink anymore,
  the mice catch the cats
  and the dogs flee from the hares,
  when the sky is covered by boards,
  sugar is bitter and pepper sweet,
  the ocean full of plants and the mountains full of water:
  then my sorrows will end.

The crickets will play at fencing,
  and the donkeys dance on tightropes,
  the hunters become monkeys
  and onion bulbs grow grape vines,

quando la luna sarà al giorno lumine
e che di gelo vestirassi il fulmine,
i dì d'Agosto saran più che friggidi
prima ch'il pianto cessi a questi occhi humidi.
Quando le capre canteranno musica,
   il dì di Pasqua sarà in giorno venere,
   i ciavatini leggeranno fisica
   e dopo pranso si darà la cenere,
   quando gli cani non havran testicoli
   e le campagne diveranno vicoli:
   al hor per te, mio volto crudelissimo,
   il cor che langue sarà felicissimo.

the moon will shine during the day
and lightening clad itself in ice,
the days of August will be very cold
before the weeping of these wet eyes will cease.
When the goats sing music,
   Easter falls on a Friday,
   the cobblers teach physics,
   one offers ashes after dinner,
   when dogs no longer have testicles,
   and the meadows become side streets:
   then, lady of the most cruel countenance,
   the heart that languishes for your sake will be completely happy.

Comment. Seconda parte, line 3, "simia" is a variant of "scimmia."

9. *Quando'io volsi l'altra sera*

Quand'io volsi l'altra sera
   restar teco in sino a dì,
   mi facesti la brusca cera
   ne volesti dir di sì
   con scusarti ch'a quattro hore
   aspetavi un gran signore.
Hoggi poi m'è stato detto,
   da persona che lo sa,
   che tu sola andasti a letto,
   dopo ch'io partì di la,
   e dormisti con tuoi guai,
   quel signor non venne mai.
Hor io penso molto bene
   la cagion qual si di ciò,
   dirò forsi com'aviene:
   quel signor se lo scordò
   e volendo a te venire,
   hebbe sonno e ando a dormire.
Ma quest'altra opinione
   calza meglio per mia fè,
   che per tua riputione
   tu dicesti così a me
   per mostrar signora mia
   ch'hai gran folla in pescharia.
Non sia ben gettarsi via,
   ne chiamar chi se ne va,
   che la troppo cortesia
   nelle donne è vanità,
   il mercante ch'altri prega
   fa vergogna alla botega.
Ma il far sempre repugnanza
   e quel sempre dir di no,
   veramente è brutta usanza
   che soffrir più non si può,
   ed è cosa da curiale
   voler sempre il memoriale.
Quando siamo tra noi soli
   tu fai più difficolta
   che non hebber gli spagnoli
   nell'impresa di Breda.
   Non v'è teco altro rimedio
   che pigliarti per assedio.

When I wished, the other evening,
   to stay with you until day,
   you gave me a tart look,
   and wouldn't say "yes,"
   with the excuse that at four,
   you were expecting some great lord.
Today I've heard,
   from a person who knows,
   that you went to bed alone
   after I left,
   and slept only with your own groans;
   the lord never came.
Now, I believe I know
   a reason for all this.
   I'll tell you what may have happened:
   the lord forgot,
   and, though wishing to come see you,
   grew sleepy and went to bed.
But another view
   is more likely, I think:
   that it was on account of your reputation
   that you said this to me,
   to show me, my lady,
   that you have a lot of fish in your pond.
It would not be good to cast oneself away,
   nor to call back a person who's departing—
   for an excess of courtesy
   in women is vanity,
   and the merchant who begs people to buy
   shames his own shop.
But always putting people off,
   and this business of always saying "no,"
   really are stupid practices,
   which can't be put up with any more,
   and it is only courtiers
   who are always wanting a memorial.
When we're alone together,
   you give me more resistance
   than the Spanish ever had
   in the conquest of Breda.
   With you there's no solution
   but to take you by siege.

Io che son poco soldato
   alla fin ti lascierò
   s'ho da star sempre in steccato
   in Venetia andar men vo
   ove almeno a tutte l'hore
   non s'aspetta quel signore.

10. *Menti, lingua bugiarda*

Prima parte
Menti, lingua bugiarda,
   di rio veleno infetta
   maladetta,
   che di fiamma novella 'l mio cor arda.
   E voi, anima mia,
   troppo credula sete.
   Ah, non sapete
   quant'habbian forza de vostr'occhi i rai!
   V'amo, mio cor, e v'amo più che mai.

Seconda parte
Ch'io delle voglie fide
   volga ad altra bellezza
   la fermezza
   o ch'altra fiamma nel mio sen s'anide?
   Lingua bugiarda, menti!
   Troppo dolce è 'l penare,
   troppo son care
   le fiamme che versate, amati rai!
   V'amo, mio bene, e v'amo più che mai.

Terza parte
Quanto più splende il sole
   delle minute stelle,
   frà le belle
   splendon le vostre luci rare e sole.
   Ah, ben degno sarei
   di sempiterno horrore
   se 'l fido core
   togliessi a si vivaci e cari rai!
   V'amo, mia speme, e v'amo più che mai.

Quarta parte
S'io v'abbandono mai,
   leggiadrissimi lumi,
   si consumi
   l'anima infida in sempiterni guai.
   Tutti nel petto mio
   versi dal foco eterno
   il crudo Averno
   d'empie fiamme penosi aspri tormenti!
   Menti, lingua bugiarda, menti, menti!

11. *Hor ch'è tempo di dormire*

Hor ch'è tempo di dormire
   dormi figlio e non vagire
   perché tempo ancor verrà
   che vagir bisognerà.
     Deh ben mio deh cor mio fà
     fa la nina nina na.

I, not being much of a soldier,
   will leave you in the end,
   if I have to stand in the lists for long;
   I'll go to Venice
   where at least they're not always
   waiting for that lord.

You lie, mendacious tongue,
   in the cruel shackles of evil
   poison,
   that my heart could burn with a new flame.
   And you, my soul,
   you are too credulous.
   Ah, you do not know
   how much power the rays of your eyes have!
   I love you, my heart, and I love you more than ever.

That I, from this faithful longing,
   could turn towards another beauty
   my steadfastness,
   or that another flame could nest in my breast?
   You lie, mendacious tongue!
   Too sweet is the suffering,
   too dear are
   the flames that you emit, beloved eyes!
   I love you, my dear, and I love you more than ever.

As the sun shines more brightly
   than the small stars,
   among all beauties
   shine your rare and exceptional eyes.
   Ah, I would well deserve
   everlasting consternation
   if I tore my faithful heart
   from such vivid and dear eyes!
   I love you, my hope, and I love you more than ever.

If I ever abandon you,
   fairest lights,
   may my unfaithful soul
   consume itself in everlasting cries.
   Into my breast
   may cruel Hell
   pour all of its eternal fire,
   the harsh torments of painful, pitiless flames!
   You lie, mendacious tongue, you lie, you lie!

Now that it is time to sleep,
   sleep, son, and don't cry;
   for the time will come soon enough
   when crying is needed.
     O my dearest, my heart:
     lullaby and sleep now.

Chiudi quei lumi divini
   come fan gl'altri bambini
   perché tosto oscuro velo
   priverà di lume il cielo.
      Deh ben mio deh cor mio fà
      fa la nina nina na.
Over prendi questo latte
   dalle mie mammelle intatte
   perché ministro crudele
   ti prepara aceto e fiele.
      Deh ben mio deh cor mio fa
      fa la nina nina na.
Amor mio sia questo petto
   hor per te morbido letto
   pria che rendi ad alta voce
   l'alma al Padre su la croce.
      Deh ben mio deh cor mio fà
      fa la nina nina na.
Posa hor queste membra belle
   vezzosette e tenerelle
   perché puoi feri e catene
   gli daran acerbe pene.
      Deh ben mio deh cor mio fa
      fa la nina nina na.
Queste mani e questi piedi
   ch'hor con gusto e gaudio vedi
   ahime, com'in varii modi
   passeran acuti chiodi!
Questa facia gratiosa
   rubiconda hor più che rosa
   sputi e schiaffi sporcheranno
   con tormento e grand'affanno.
Ah con quanto tuo dolore
   sola speme del mio core
   questo capo e questi crini
   passeran acuti spini.
Ah ch'in questo divin petto
   amor mio dolce e diletto
   vi farà piaga mortale
   empia lancia e disleale.
Dormi dunque figlio mio,
   dormi pur Redentor mio,
   perché poi con lieto viso
   si vedrem in Paradiso.
Hor che dormi la mia vita
   del mio cor gioia compita
   tacia ogn'un con puro zelo
   tacian sin la terra e 'l Cielo.
E fra tanto io che farò?
   Il mio ben contemplerò
   ne starò col capo chino
   sin che dorme il mio Bambino.

Close those divine eyes
   as other babies do;
   for soon a dark veil
   will deprive the sky of light
      O my dearest, my heart:
      lullaby and sleep now.
Or take this milk
   from my immaculate breasts;
   for a cruel magistrate
   is preparing vinegar and gall for you.
      O my dearest, my heart:
      lullaby and sleep now.
My love, let this breast
   be now a soft bed for you,
   before, with a loud voice, you give
   your soul to the Father, on the cross.
      O my dearest, my heart:
      lullaby and sleep now.
Rest now your beautiful small limbs,
   so charming and delicate;
   for later, irons and chains
   will cause them bitter pains.
      O my dearest, my heart:
      lullaby and sleep now.
These hands and feet,
   which now you behold with zest and joy—
   alas, in how many ways
   will sharp nails pierce them!
This graceful face,
   ruddier than a rose—
   spitting and slaps will defile it
   with torture and great suffering.
Ah, with how much pain for you,
   O only hope of my heart,
   this head and this brow
   will be pierced by sharp thorns.
For in this divine breast,
   O my sweet and delightful love,
   an impious traitorous spear
   will make a mortal wound.
Sleep, therefore, my son,
   sleep then, my Savior,
   for later with joyful faces
   we'll see each other in Paradise.
Now that you are sleeping, O my life,
   O complete joy of my heart,
   let all be quiet with pure zeal,
   even the earth and the heavens.
Meanwhile, what shall I do?
   I will watch my dear,
   not letting my head bow
   as long as my baby sleeps.

12. Chi vuol ch'io m'innamori

Chi vuol ch'io m'innamori
   mi dic'almen di che?
   Se d'animati fiori
   un fiore, che cosa è?
   Se di begli occhi ardenti
   ah, che sian tosto spenti?

Whoever wants me to fall in love,
   tell me at least—with what?
   If I should fall in love with lively flowers,
   what is a flower?
   If with beautiful passionate eyes,
   ah, that will soon be extinguished?

La morte, ohime, n'uccide,	Death, alas, kills them,
il tempo il tutto frange:	Time destroys everything:
hoggi si ride	today we laugh,
e puoi diman si piange.	and then tomorrow we weep.
Se vuol ch'un auro crine	If I should be bound
mi leghi, e che sarà,	by golden hair, what will happen,
se di gelate brine	when freezing cold
quel or si spargerà?	shatters that gold?
La neve del bel seno,	The snow of a beautiful breast,
qual neve ancor, vien meno.	just like real snow, fades.
La morte ancor produce	Death will cause
terror, ch'il seno ingombra.	terror to fill the heart.
Hoggi siam luce	Today we are light
e poi diman siam ombra.	and then tomorrow we are shadow.
Dovrò prezzar tesori	Should I care for riches
se vedo io morirò?	if I can see that I will die?
E ricercar honori	And seek honors
che presto io lascierò?	that I will soon leave behind?
In che fondar mia speme	In what should I put my hope
se giongon l'hore estreme?	when the final hours come?
Ohime, che mai si pasce	Woe, to those who satisfy
di vanitade il core!	their hearts with vanity!
Hoggi si nasce,	Today we are born,
e poi diman si muore.	and tomorrow we die.

13. Un bambin che và alla scola

Un bambin che và alla scola	A child that goes to school
fatto son, ohime, meschin,	I have become, alas, poor me,
ond'Amor m'ha preso a folla	and so Love has led me on
come fus un passerin.	as though I were a little sparrow.
Quel ch'è peggio, è che la puta	What's worse is that the girl
che m'in segna l'alfabet	who teaches me the alphabet
d'ogni mal sempre m'inputa	always charges me with mischief
e s'acorda col fraschet.	and confirms her point with the switch.
Un uccel che sta nel bosco	A bird that lives in the forest
fatto son, ohime, meschin,	I have been made, alas, poor me,
ond'Amor col fiele e tosco	so that Love, with gall and poison,
m'ha inescato il saracin.	has baited and trapped me.
Quel ch'è peggio, è ch'il crudele	What is worse is that the cruel one
privo m'ha di libertà.	has robbed me of liberty.
E con lagrime, e querele	With only tears and complaints
vivrò sempre in poverta.	I will always live in poverty.
Duro sasso a presso un rio	A hard rock next to a river
fatto son, ohime, meschin,	I have been made, alas, poor me,
onde l'acqua de l'oblio	so that to drink continuously
bevo ogn'hor, per mio destin.	the water of oblivion is my destiny.
Quel ch'è peggio, è ch'ho nel petto	What's worse is that in my breast
vivo incendio, e grave ardor,	I have a vivid burning and grave ardor,
che mi fa tanto soggetto	that makes me so defenseless
che languendo, pero ogn'hor.	that, languishing, I perish unceasingly.
Come cera apo del foco	Like wax next to the fire
mi consumo, ohime, meschin,	I am consumed, alas, poor me,
e mancando a poco a poco	and, failing little by little,
alla fossa vuo vicin.	I am nearing my grave.
Quel ch'è peggio, e mi dispiace,	What's worse and what displeases me so,
che restiate voi qua su,	is that you will remain up here,
onde prego Amor rapace,	therefore I ask predatory Cupid
ch'anco voi parta la giù.	that he may send you down here, too.

14. *El me tira nott'e dì*

El me tira nott'e dì	He assaults me night and day
con la saetta,	with his arrow,
Amor furbetta,	cunning little Love,
ma spero un giorno	but I hope
di far ritorno	to return one day
nel mio primiero stato.	to my first state.
Ah, son piagato!	Ah, I am wounded!
El me tira notte, e dì	He assaults me night and day
con l'arco, e strale	with bow and arrow
e mi fa male,	and hurts me,
ma spero maga	but I place my hope in a witch
che la mia piaga	who will restore my wound
ritorni a miglior stato.	to a better state.
Ah, son piagato!	Ah, I am wounded!
El me tira notte, e dì	He assaults me night and day
col fero dardo	with his fierce dart
ond'io tutto ardo,	so that I burn all over
ma spero aita	but I hope for help
alla ferita	for my injury
et al mio cor sprezzato.	and for my scorned heart.
Ah, son piagato!	Ah, I am wounded!
El me tira notte, e dì	He assaults me night and day
senza far tregua	without making a truce
e 'l sen dilegua,	and he makes my heart fail,
ma spero forsi	but I hope maybe,
se troppo corsi,	once I have tried long enough,
ritrar il pie legato.	that I will be able to draw back my tied foot.
O sfortunato!	O unfortunate me!

15. *Non ha 'l regno d'amor*

Non ha 'l regno d'amor	There is no one in the kingdom of love
più felice di me, no, alla fe!	more blessed than I, no, by my faith!
Vivo lieto nel cor, sento ogn'hor	I live with a happy heart, I feel always
un contento, un piacer, un pensier	a contentment, a pleasure, a thought
dolc'e car che mi sprona ad amar.	so sweet and dear that spurs me to love.
O che dolce dilet	Oh, with what sweet delight
mi trabocca nel sen! Vengo men,	my breast overflows! I am failing,
e col canto, e col suon, in canzon	and yet melodiously I sing canzone
canto rime e strambot, giorno, e not,	rime and strambotti day and night,
o che car viver lieto, e danzar.	O how wonderful to live and dance so happily.
Che soave gioir	What sweet pleasure it is
e l'amar, e goder! Quest'è 'l ver,	to love and enjoy! This is the truth,
e godendo baciar e bear	and to kiss with pleasure and to blissfully enjoy
l'alma, e 'l pet, e quel vis, paradis	this soul, this breast, and this face, the paradise
d'un'amant servo fido, e costant.	of a lover, of a faithful and constant servant.
Ah, che più non si puo!	Ah that one cannot bear more!
Per dolcezza, e content, io mi sent	I feel the sweetness and pleasure
a mancar, e finir, [e morir],	making me swoon and die.
Nel tuo petto, mio cor, caro ardor,	In your arms, my heart, my dear passion,
morte vien, a Dio, Filli mio ben.	death arrives, farewell, Phyllis, my beloved.

Comment. Second stanza, lines 3–4: the "canzona," "rima," and "strambotto" are genres of Italian lyric poetry.

16. *Sentirete una canzonetta*

Sentirete una canzonetta	You will hear a little song
sopra al bel bocchin,	about the pretty little mouth,
del mio vago, e dispietato amor	of my fair and merciless love

ch'ogn'hor nel cor mi tormenta e fa	who at all times in my heart torments me
sospirare per sua gran beltà.	and makes me sigh for the sake of her great beauty.
Sentirete un soave canto	You will hear sweet singing
sopra al bel nasin,	about the pretty little nose,
del mio vago, e dispietato amor	of my fair and merciless love
ch'ogn'hor nel cor mi tormenta e fa,	who at all times in my heart torments me
sospirare per sua gran beltà.	and makes me sigh for the sake of her great beauty.
Sentirete la doglia acerba	You will hear about the bitter pain
che mi fa morir,	that makes me die
per il vago, e dolce caro ben	For my fair and sweet dear treasure
ch'ogn'hor nel cor mi tormenta e fa,	who at all times in my heart torments me
sospirare per sua gran beltà.	and makes me sigh for the sake of her great beauty.
Sentirete d'amor la piaga	You will hear about the love wound
che mi fa languir	that makes me languish
per un ciglio dispietato, e fer	for a merciless and fierce face
ch'ogn'hor d'ardor mi tormenta e fa,	who at all times through my ardor torments me
sospirare ma non ha pietà.	and makes me sigh, but has no pity.
Sentirete per chioma d'oro	You will hear how, because of golden hair,
che son gionto al fin,	I have come to the end,
belle treccie, ma spietate, si,	beautiful tresses, but pitiless, yes,
ch'ogn'hor il cor m'allacciate, ohime,	who at all times, bind my heart, alas,
che ne godo ma non so perché.	in such a way that I enjoy it without knowing why.

Plate 1. Tarquinio Merula, *Curtio precipitato et altri capricii* (1638), title page. Courtesy of the Governing Body of Christ Church, Oxford, Mus. 795(7).

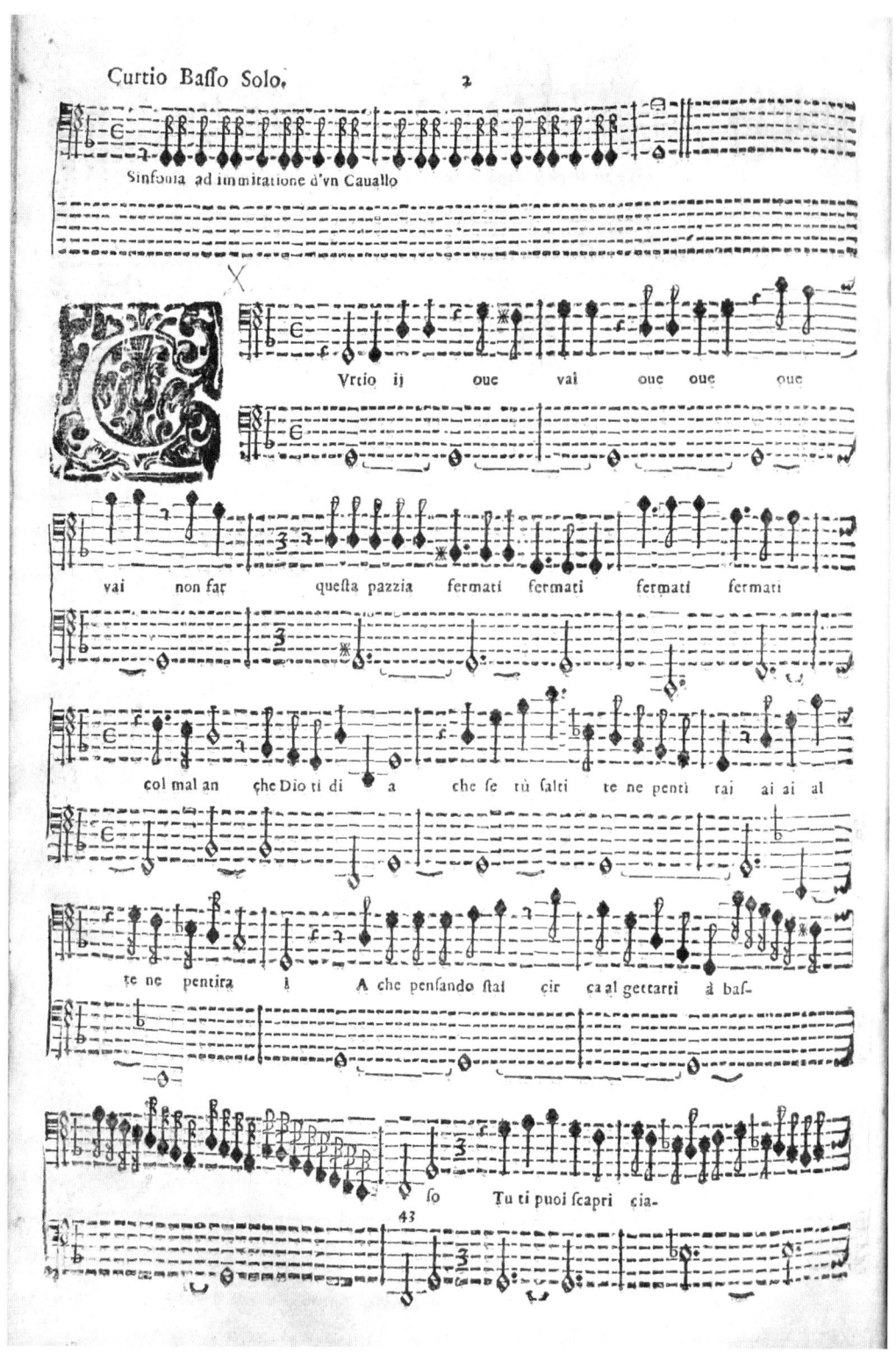

Plate 2. Tarquinio Merula, *Curtio precipitato et altri capricii* (1638), first page of "Curtio, ove vai?" Courtesy of the Governing Body of Christ Church, Oxford, Mus. 795(7).

Curtio precipitato et altri capricii

Dedication

Ill[ustrissi]mo Signor | Mio Sig[no]re et Padron Col[endissi]mo

Marco Curtio Giovane Romano, come paia corto di nome, la fama però l'inalza alle stelle. Per pietà della Patria si dannó egli nel seno delli Empij: Ma la Religione dè grati Cittadini l'honorò qual'Idea di carità, più degno di vita immortale, che se mai havesse provato morte. Meritò di sopravivere al sepolcro; perche sepellissi volontario prima di morire. Quindi non patisce la mia Musa che giaccia in silentio trà Furie discordanti, un che acquetò il furore d'Apolline irato: E con novi concerti il sottrahe dall'Inferno dell'oblivione un altro Orfeo; ch'appunto dietro à se trasse rupi, quando riuní caduto quel foro del foro di Roma. Ch'involino le tenebre d'ignoranza quelli, che l'infette nubi tolse dalla faccia della terra? anzi più di Teseo salutare alli huomeni merita dalli huomeni un' Hercole, che dalla forza delli habitanti di Lete á questa nostra luce il rapporti. V[ostra] S[ignoria] Illustrissima é quella, il cui valore l'assomiglia ad Alcide, mentre vi degna nell' Arma paterna d'una delle prime insegne del Tebano. Le stelle poi, e'l chiaro che v'illustra sovra tante la Famiglia come non levaranno da cupi profondi, che merita nostra superior luce? Sù che le musiche scienze honorando alletareste insin Proserpina, e Pluto á darvi in gratia i schiavi più stretti. Cosi ella con occhio benigno favorisca questi miei Componimenti, che Curtio precipitato no[n] cura d'altro sollevamento, [ed] i Capricci abbastanza restano acreditati di prudenza, le fò humilissima riverenza. Di Venetia il Primo Zugno.

Di V[ostra] S[ignoria] Illustrissima Devotissimo [ed] obligatissimo Serv[itore] Il Cavalier Tarquinio Merula

Most Illustrious Lord, my Most Exalted Lord and Patron

Marcus Curtius the Roman youth, although by name would appear to be short, was however elevated to the stars by fame. For the love of his Country he damned himself among the sinners. But the religion of his grateful fellow citizens honored him as an ideal of charity, more worthy of an immortal life than if he had experienced death. He deserved to survive beyond the grave because he buried himself voluntarily before experiencing death. Therefore, my Muse cannot allow the one who placated the ire of an enraged Apollo to lie in silence in the midst of the fighting Furies. And with new concerti, a new Orpheus takes out of the Hell of oblivion him who brought rocks down with him when, having fallen he closed the hole in the Roman Forum. Should those who have been taken from the face of the Earth by the poisonous clouds be the ones to dispel the darkness of ignorance? I think rather that someone more beneficial to his fellow men than Theseus was, deserves to have a new Hercules come, who will take him from the stronghold of the inhabitants of Lethe back to our light. Your Most Illustrious Lordship is the one whose valor resembles that of Hercules, while in your coat of arms one of the first insignia of the Theban ennobles you. How could the stars and the fame that make your Family illustrious over so many others not bring out from the deep darkness him who deserves to see our light above? In honoring the musical sciences you would entertain even Proserpina and Pluto so that they would give you their dearest slaves as a gift. Thus, with your benign eye, may you favor these compositions, since my fallen Curtius does not care about any other praise, and the capricci are credited with sufficient prudence, I humbly bow to you. In Venice, on the first of June.

The most devout and most grateful servant of Your Most Illustrious Lordship, Cavalier Tarquinio Merula

Dedicatory Sonnets

Sonetto. | Del Molto Ill[ustre] Signor D. Claudio Sachelli, L'Avido. | Al Sig[nor] Cavalier Tarquinio Merula, per il suo Curtio.

Curtio al morir s'affretta? E tù col canto
   Affrettando le note i passi aiuti
   Sprona il destrier? E tù con cento acuti
   Colpi lo sproni à rovinoso pianto.
Ma pietoso pur' anco il freni alquanto;
   Se ben le voci tue, par ch'ei rifiuti
   Ei mor precipitando; e mille aiuti
   Ha da te, che profondi i tuoni in tanto.
Cedati pur chi da gli oscuri Inferni
   Credea goder la Donna al canto uscita,
   E rapirla di nuovo à i fati eterni.
A più felice sorte il Ciel t'invita,
   Se ne la morte altrui te stesso eterni,
   E s'ella ha dal tuo canto eterna vita.

From the Most illustrious Signor Don Claudio Sachelli, The Avid. To Signor Cavalier Tarquinio Merula, for his Curtio.

   Curtio rushes to his death? And you rushing your notes in singing help him to get there. He spurs on his horse? And you with a hundred high notes spur him to ruinous tears.

   But at times, moved by pity, you slow him down somewhat; though it seems he is not heeding your voices, he dies by falling, and he is helped by you a thousand times, since you get down so low in your notes.

   He should indeed bow to you, taken out from dark Hades, believed to be able to enjoy his woman, by this song, and rescued from the eternal fate. Heaven invites you to a happier fate, if you make yourself eternal [by singing of] someone else's death, and if she from your song receives eternal life.

Sonetto. | Del Molto Illustre Sig[nor] Cav[alier] Roberto Poggiolini, | All'istesso Autore

Canti chi vuol del Cittaredo Ebreo
    Ch'in Saul frenò spirto al suon dei carmi,
    Vanti pur se prevalse il Tracio Orfeo
    Qual suonator del plettro à trattar l'armi;
Siasi chi sà dell'Aracinto Atteo
    Mille prove cantando in cor dettarmi,
    Vaglia chi puó dell'Africano Anteo
    Con Encomi eternar metalli, e marmi,
Che la palma à me vien sortita intanto
    Per di CETRA toccarl'alto, él profondo,
    MERULA, ò mio TARQUINIO offrirti il canto;
E dir ch'altri à te sol dato è secondo,
    E dir, che sovra altrui tu porti il vanto,
    Miracolo il maggior, stupor del Mondo.

Sonnet of the Most Illustrious Signor Cavalier Roberto Poggiolini, to the same author

Let others sing of the Hebrew harpist who tamed the spirit of Saul with the sound of his poems. Let the Thracian Orpheus be proud that he prevailed over arms by playing his plectrum.

Let there be those who can sing to my heart of the thousand exploits of Amphion. Let those who can, make the name of the African Antheus eternal in metal and marble.

I, meanwhile, have the chance to give a prize for the high and low notes of the lyre, Merula, o my Tarquinio, and I offer you a song;

and say that others can only come second to you, and that you are above all others, O most great miracle and wonder of the world!

1. Curtio, ove vai?

2. Fiori, fiori, o quanti fiori

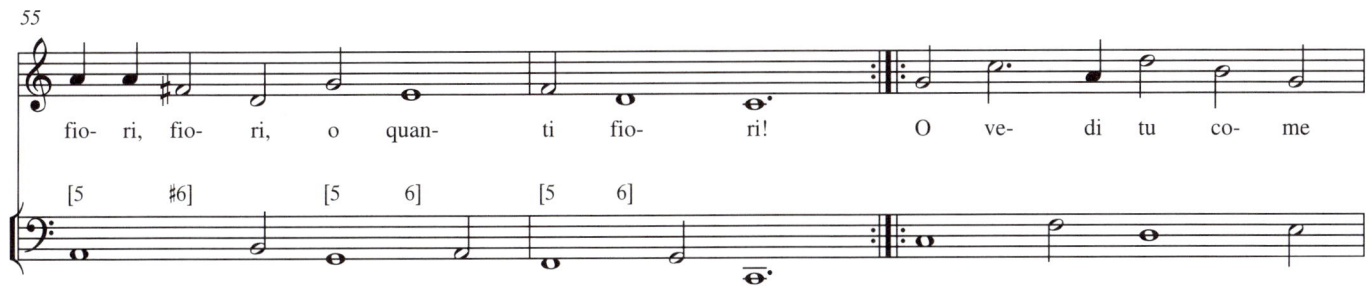
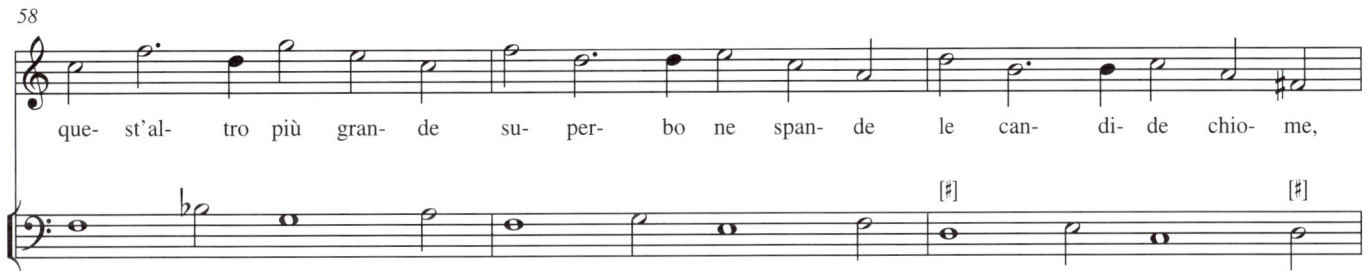
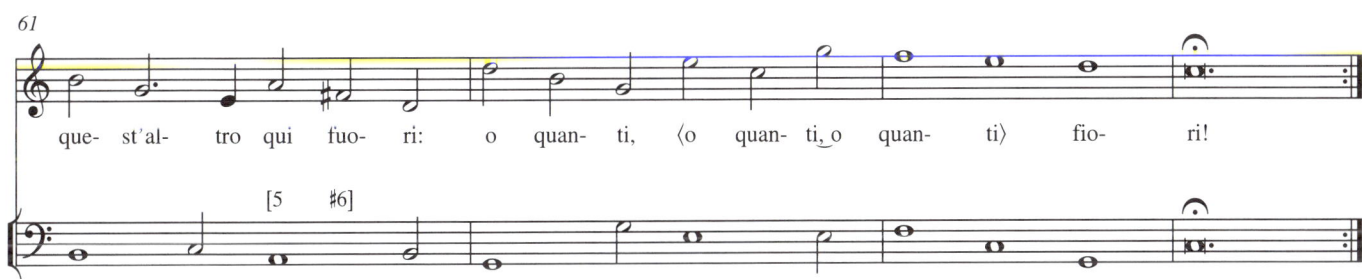

3. Folle è ben che si crede

Pio di Savoia

2. Altri per gelosia
　spiri pur empie fiamme dal seno
　versi pure Megera il veneno
　perché rompi al mio ben la fede mia.
　Morte il viver mi toglia
　mai sia ver che si scioglia
　quel caro laccio che preso m'ha.
　Dica chi vuole, dica chi sa.

3. Ben havrò tempo, e loco
　da sfogar l'amorose mie pene
　da temprar de l'amato mio bene
　e de l'arso mio cor, l'occulto foco,
　e tra l'ombre, e gli orrori
　de notturni splendori
　il mio ben furto s'asconderà.
　Dica chi vuole, dica chi sa.

4. Conza lavez e colder

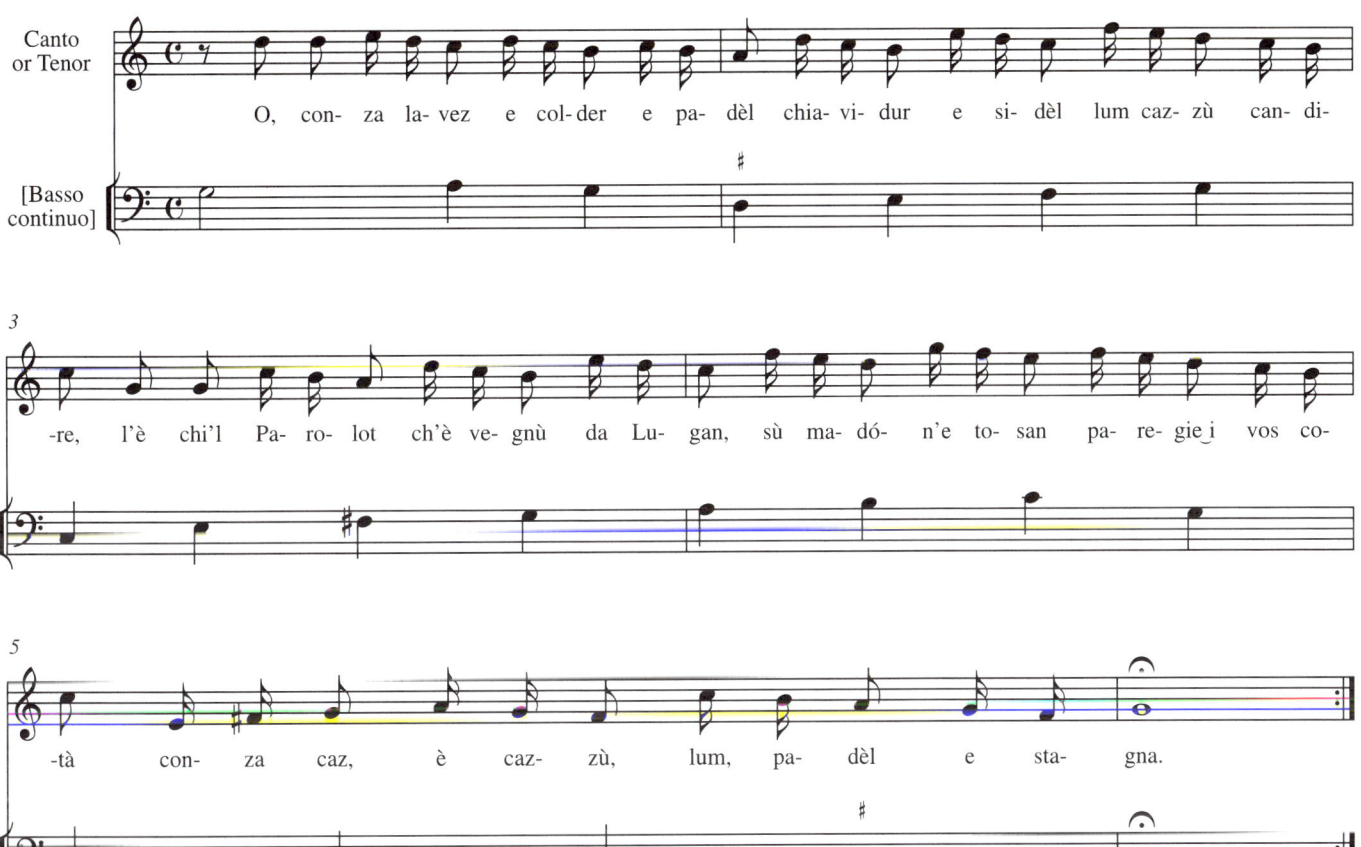

2. I' ho bon stagnado bona lima martel
mantisit tinivel, e cient'olter meste
se ghiss ou quai vas che fus rot, ò fes dan,
non ve ste met affan, laghe ved portè scia
conza caz, è cazzù, lum, padèl e stagna.

3. Affeda ch'aù sciur se vöapi ch'aù lavora
ch'in mane de mez'hora vuoi faù stravede
e si no v' content'à reson, e mesura
vuoi perd la facchiura, el vos dagn' vuoi refa
conza caz, è cazzù, lum, padèl e stagna.

4. Per cünt del mercà dan' vu la sentenza
ch'au sciur inconsienza de sta al vos parè
e s' n'hissou quatrin cosi in pront, ve promet
de sav' anch'asper, sin che mi torno à passà
conza caz, è cazzù, lum, padèl e stagna.

5. Fronte st'occasion tant che son paregia
che san' consorà da rial coldire
e si non' do gust con si bella destrezza
de fau per dolcezza romagn'incanta
cacciem pur i sù forch', e mandem à inpica.

5. Sempre lieta, gioconda, e brillante

2. Se la ride, o la balla o canta,
   se la scherza, la guarda o lavora,
   la rapisce, la lega, l'incanta,
   la ferisce, l'accend'e innamora;
   ogn'un l'ama, la serva, e l'adora,
   ch'ella è troppo gustosa, e carina,
   la mia cara, amorosa Dorina.

3. Mai si turba, si sdegna, o s'adira,
   mai si mostra ritrosa, o rubella;
   anzi ascolta, gradisse, e rimira,
   compatisce, e cortese favella.
   Quanto è vaga, mirabile, e bella!
   Tanto è dolce gustosa mamina
   la mia cara diletta Dorina.

4. Gioia, gusto, piacer, e diletto,
   gaudio, pace, dolcezza, e contento
   spira e porge quel viso, e quel petto,
   quel leggiadro e gentil portamento.
   Ahi ch'al cielo rapire mi sento,
   quando miro, e vagheggio vicina
   la mia cara adorata Dorina!

6. Un pastorel nato non so

2. Belva non è ch'al lo suo stral
   schermir possa, o fuggire
   ne pari a se braccio mortal
   si vidde mai colpire
   ma d'amar, ma d'amar non vuol sentire,
   sono i canti, sono i pianti sparsi in van.

3. Cupido al fin quel grand'arcier
   trionfante de cori
   al cui divin alto poter
   cedon gli eccelsi chori
   affrenar, affrenar penso i furori
   di si altiere, di si fiero, spiritel.

4. Ma vinto ancor restò non men
   l'angiolin faretrato
   e di tremor sparso, e ripien
   gridò mercè prostrato,
   el pastor, el pastor vago, e spietato
   d'arco e strali, sin del'ali lo spogliò.

5. Hor chi potrà già mai spiegar
   tal beltà si proterva,
   s'amor non ha per contrastar
   arma che più le serva?
   fugg'ogn'alm, fugg'ogn'alma come cerva
   ch'è s'è gionta, ch'è s'è punta guai a fe.

7. Non mi chiedete, o fidi amici

2. Dama ch'adoro ha sparso il crine
  nel laberinto del mio core,
  le cui luci peregrine
  al sol furan lo splendore.
  Mi tormenta e fa languir
  e non gliel posso dir.

3. Deh, se puo mai sentir conforto!
  Ignudo spirto io prego almeno
  che dopo ch'io sarò morto
  mi fia tratto il cor dal seno,
  ch'ivi ogn'un potra scoprir
  ciò ch'hor non posso dir.

4. La bella imago, el gentil nome,
  dolce cagion de la mia morte
  qui vedransi al hor, e come
  fe tacermi invida sorte
  e forzommi al fin morir
  per non poter lo dir.

8. Quando gli uccelli porteranno i zoccoli
Canzonetta in sdrucciolo

9. Quand'io volsi l'altra sera

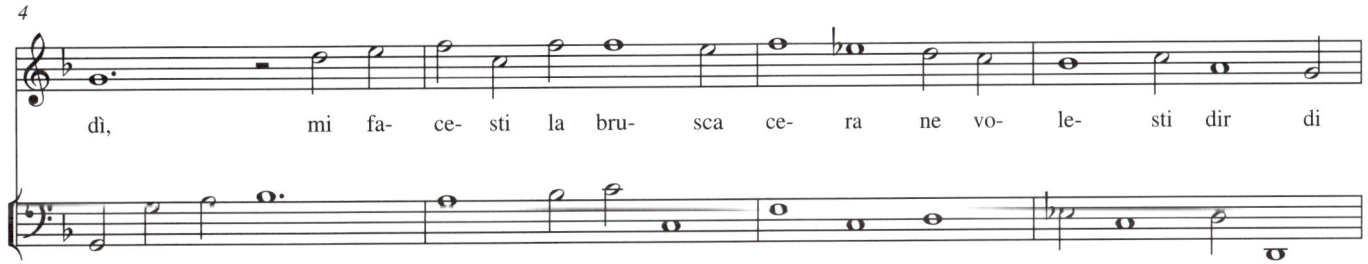
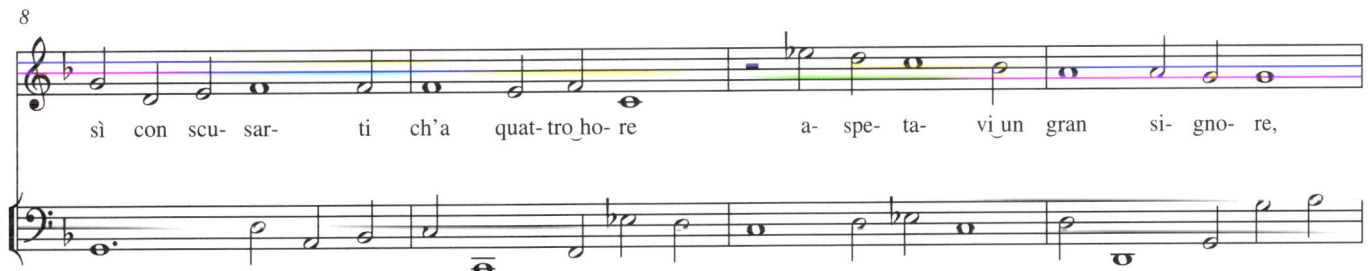

2. Hoggi poi m'è stato detto,
   da persona che lo sa,
   che tu sola andasti a letto,*
   dopo ch'io partì di la,
   e dormisti con tuoi guai,
   quel signor non venne mai.

3. Hor io penso molto bene
   la cagion qual si di ciò,
   dirò forsi com'aviene:
   quel signor se lo scordò
   e volendo a te venire,
   hebbe sonno e ando a dormire.

4. Ma quest'altra opinione
   calza meglio per mia fè,
   che per tua riputione
   tu dicesti così a me
   per mostrar signora mia
   ch'hai gran folla in pescharia.

5. Non sia ben gettarsi via,
   ne chiamar chi se ne va,
   che la troppo cortesia
   nelle donne è vanità,
   il mercante ch'altri prega
   fa vergogna alla botega.

6. Ma il far sempre repugnanza
   e quel sempre dir di no,
   veramente è brutta usanza
   che soffrir più non si può,
   ed è cosa da curiale
   voler sempre il memoriale.

7. Quando siamo tra noi soli
   tu fai più difficoltà
   che non hebber gli spagnoli
   nell'impresa di Breda.
   Non v'è teco altro rimedio
   che pigliarti per assedio.

8. Io che son poco soldato
   alla fin ti lascierò
   s'ho da star sempre in steccato
   in Venetia andar men vo
   ove almeno a tutte l'hore
   non s'aspetta quel signore.

*In this and each subsequent stanza the third syllable of this line may be extended over two notes to match the musical setting.

10. Menti, lingua bugiarda

11. Hor ch'è tempo di dormire

Canzonetta spirituale sopra alla nanna

12. Chi vuol ch'io m'innamori

Canzonetta spirituale

Chi vuol ch'io m'innamori mi dic'al men di che? Se d'animati fiori un fiore, che cosa è? Se di begli occhi ardenti ah, che sian tosto spenti? La morte, ohime, n'uccide, il tempo il tutto frange: hoggi si ride e puoi diman si piange, hoggi si ride e puoi diman si piange.

2. Se vuol ch'un auro crine
mi leghi, e che sarà,
se di gelate brine
quel or si spargerà?
La neve del bel seno,
qual neve ancor, vien meno.
La morte ancor produce
terror, ch'il seno ingombra.
Hoggi siam luce
e poi diman siam ombra.

3. Dovrò prezzar tesori
se vedo io morirò?
E ricercar honori
che presto io lascierò?
In che fondar mia speme
se giongon l'hore estreme?
Ohime, che mai si pasce
di vanitade il core!
Hoggi si nasce,
e poi diman si muore.

13. Un bambin che và alla scola

2. Un uccel che sta nel bosco
   fatto son, ohime, meschin,
   ond'Amor col fiele e tosco
   m'ha inescato il saracin.
   Quel ch'è peggio, è ch'il crudele
   privo m'ha di libertà.
   E con lagrime, e querele
   vivrò sempre in poverta.

3. Duro sasso a presso un rio
   fatto son, ohime, meschin,
   onde l'acqua de l'oblio
   bevo ogn'hor, per mio destin.
   Quel ch'è peggio, è ch'ho nel petto
   vivo incendio, e grave ardor,
   che mi fa tanto soggetto
   che languendo, pero ogn'hor.

4. Come cera apo del foco
   mi consumo, ohime, meschin,
   e mancando a poco a poco
   alla fossa vuo vicin.
   Quel ch'è peggio, e mi dispiace,
   che restiate voi qua su,
   onde prego Amor rapace,
   ch'anco voi parta la giù.

14. El me tira nott'e dì

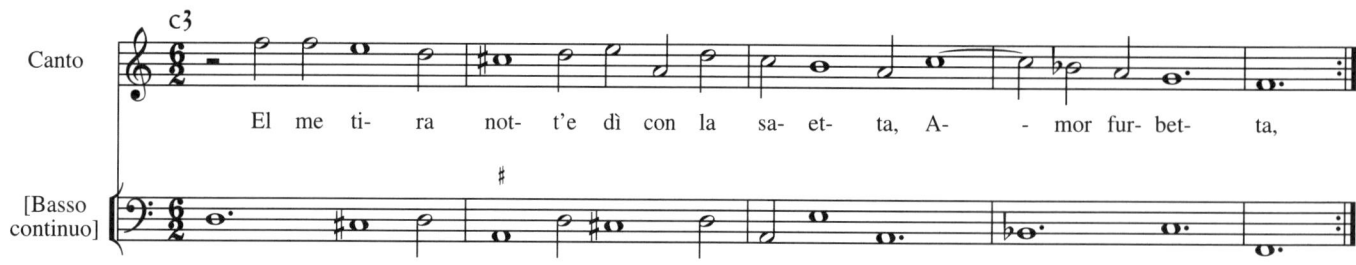

2. El me tira notte, e dì
   con l'arco, e strale
   e mi fa male,
   ma spero maga
   che la mia piaga
   ritorni a miglior stato.
   Ah, son piagato!

3. El me tira notte, e dì
   col fero dardo
   ond'io tutto ardo,
   ma spero aita
   alla ferita
   et al mio cor sprezzato.
   Ah, son piagato!

4. El me tira notte, e dì
   senza far tregua
   e 'l sen dilegua,
   ma spero forsi
   se troppo corsi,
   ritrar il pie legato.
   O sfortunato!

15. Non ha 'l regno d'amor

2. O che dolce dilet
   mi trabocca nel sen! Vengo men,
   e col canto, e col suon, in canzon
   canto rime e strambot, giorno, e not,
   o che car viver lieto, e danzar.

3. Che soave gioir
   e l'amar, e goder! Quest'è 'l ver,
   e godendo baciar e bear
   l'alma, e 'l pet, e quel vis, paradis
   d'un'amant servo fido, e costant.

4. Ah, che più non si puo!
   Per dolcezza, e content, io mi sent
   a mancar, e finir, [e morir],
   Nel tuo petto, mio cor, caro ardor,
   morte vien, a Dio, Filli mio ben.

16. Sentirete una canzonetta

2. Sentirete un soave canto
   sopra al bel nasin,
   del mio vago, e dispietato amor
   ch'ogn'hor nel cor mi tormenta e fa,
   sospirare per sua gran beltà.

3. Sentirete la doglia acerba
   che mi fa morir,
   per il vago, e dolce caro ben
   ch'ogn'hor nel cor mi tormenta e fa,
   sospirare per sua gran beltà.

4. Sentirete d'amor la piaga
   che mi fa languir
   per un ciglio dispietato, e fer
   ch'ogn'hor d'ardor mi tormenta e fa,
   sospirare ma non ha pietà.

5. Sentirete per chioma d'oro
   che son gionto al fin,
   belle treccie, ma spietate, si,
   ch'ogn'hor il cor m'allacciate, ohime,
   che ne godo ma non so perché.

Critical Report

Editorial Methods

This edition is based on Tarquinio Merula's *Curtio precipitato et altri capricii,* published by Magni in Venice, 1638. The original is held by Christ Church Library, Oxford University, Mus 795(7). The ordering and titling of works follows the original source, in which *capoversi* are used as titles in the *tavola*. The numbering has been added tacitly, and the punctuation and orthography have been modernized, as they have in the texts. Genre labels, when they appear, are taken from the original, and multiple parts of a composition are treated as a single work.

The original F4 clefs have been retained for the voice in no. 1, "Curtio, ove vai?" and for the continuo throughout. The remainder of the pieces use C1 clefs for the voice, which have been changed to modern treble clefs. In nos. 2–6, the voice designation "canto overo tenore" suggests the option of transposition down an octave for male singers. Nos. 11–16 are designated "canto solo," while nos. 7–9 lack voice designations. This edition retains the voice designations from the source, adding "canto" in brackets for those without designation. No. 16 is unique in this volume in including an instrumental ritornello; the original C3 clef has been retained for the ritornello melody.

The key signatures from the original have all been retained, including key signature changes within a piece, with the exception of no. 11, "Hor ch'è tempo di dormire." This song conforms closely enough to modern D minor tonality to warrant adding the b♭, which appears as an accidental throughout Merula's print, to the key signature. The change of tempo in the final section, which is original, is thus also a change of key signature in the edition.

Merula uses the meter signs ₵, ₵3, and 3. The pieces and sections of pieces in ₵ have been transcribed in modern common time, retaining the original note values. Merula's use of triple meter signs is variable: he uses ₵3 and 3 interchangably, and in piece no. 1, "Curtio, ove vai?," he uses 3 to refer to two different meters. Therefore, all triple meters except those in no. 1 have been transcribed in $\frac{6}{2}$, retaining the original note values. The triple meter sections in no. 1 have also been transcribed with original note values, resulting in a $\frac{6}{4}$ time signature for measures 9–10 and 11–22, and $\frac{6}{2}$ for the remaining triple-meter sections. Throughout the edition, original triple meter signs are given above the staff.

In the original print, the placement of barlines is irregular. For ₵ passages, barlines are normally placed every two semibreves, with occasional variant lengths of one or three semibreves, and the "half measure" subdivision is clearly defined by the use of tied semibreves in the basso continuo line. Therefore, the edition adds barlines as needed in ₵ in order to regularize the measure length to one semibreve. Merula's placement of barlines within the triple-meter passages is also irregular, but in a way that is metrically (or hypermetrically) meaningful, in that it reflects Merula's manipulation of the various possibilities inherent in the versification; in the edition, the original barlines have therefore been retained, and measure lengths in these passages may be shorter or longer (usually by a half measure) than expected in modern practice. There are, however, a few cases where a printer's error seems to be the source of the irregularity, and the emendations made in these places are detailed in the critical notes.

In cases where a measure (in the edition) is divided between the end of one system and the beginning of another (in the original print), the original ties are replaced with the longer, implied note value. However, when shorter note values with ties appear in the middle of a system, the shorter values are preserved. At the end of "Curtio, ove vai?," for example, the repeated notes may have been used to encourage the continuo player(s) to reinforce the antecedent/consequent structure of the singer's echoing phrases. The groupette numerals found in piece no. 1 are placed above the notes, replacing the original notation which consists of the ratios 6:4 and 9:4 below the vocal staff. Final longas are replaced by shorter note values with fermatas as appropriate for the time signature, thus in some cases duplicating fermatas from the print and in some cases adding them. All other fermatas are original.

The stem directions, beaming patterns, and rhythmic groupings of notes and rests in the source are made to conform to modern conventions in the edition. Melismas are also beamed according to modern practice. In those cases where the source uses a slur to indicate a melisma it has been retained, but none have been added. All ornamentation has been retained from the source, and none has been added.

Merula, according to the convention of his time, used accidentals in front of each inflected note, usually excepting direct repetitions. Although not completely consistent in this practice, the intended pitch is almost always clear from context. This edition observes modern practice in which accidentals last through the measure unless cancelled. Source accidentals made redundant thereby are omitted without comment. Those cases where the original is faulty or unclear have been recorded in the critical notes, and all editorial accidentals are given in brackets before the note; those also last through the measure unless cancelled.

Repeated text shown by the idem sign *ij* in the original has been supplied in angle brackets. Editorial additions of text are shown in square brackets. The text underlay follows the source, with words divided according to modern practice. Critical notes describe original orthography that is not reproduced in the edition or covered by the global statement in the "Texts and Translations" section.

Merula's continuo is very lightly figured, as befits a free, semi-improvisatory performance practice where the accompanist and singer were often the same person. It is understood that the continuo player will respond to the vocal line when choosing harmonies. For this reason, the edition only supplies editorial figures in the case of parallel passages in the strophic variation songs, in which figures from the first stanza have been added to the subsequent stanzas. There is a potential ambiguity regarding inflected continuo figures in the source. Raised harmonies are indicated, as is customary, with a sharp sign, whether the actual inflection be sharp or natural. But when two figures appear over a single bass note, such as 5–6 or 7–6, the source continues to place the sharp sign in the staff above the bass note, rather than adjacent to a specific numeral of the figure in question. Thus, raised sixths in a 5–6 figure, for instance, are signified by the same sharp sign that might also mark a raised third above the initial harmony. An editorial decision has been made regarding each of these harmonies based on the musical context. In all cases, a raised third for 4–3 figures at cadences is understood even if not explicit in the figure. Redundant continuo figures over sustained notes have been omitted. "Sentirete una canzonetta" (no. 16) uses an unusual two-staff notation for the continuo, which at the concluding ritornello includes a melody on the upper staff. As described in the introduction, this appears to be in imitation of the drone effect created by instruments such as the hurdy-gurdy or bagpipe. The full staffing from the original has been retained, but does not necessarily indicate performance by more than one continuo instrument.

Critical Notes

The critical notes report discrepancies between the edition and the source not covered by the general editorial methods. In pitch designation, c′ is middle C. The following abbreviations are used: B = bass; C = canto; B.c. = basso continuo.

1. *Curtio, ove vai?*

M. 24, B, note 5 lacks flat.   M. 27, B, note 9 lacks flat.   M. 33, B, notes 8, 10, 12, 13, 16, semitone clash retained from original.   M. 97, the editorial additions reflect the repetition at mm. 115–16.

3. *Folle è ben che si crede*

M. 15, C, notes 4–5, "vole," stanza 1 only.   Stanza 3, line 6, word 2 is "nuturni."   Stanza 3, line 7, word 3 is "bel."

6. *Un pastorel nato non so*

Stanza 4, line 5 is "Fugg'ogn'alma, fugg'ogn'alma come cerva."

7. *Non mi chiedete, o fidi amici*

Subtitle "canzonetta" above initial.   Stanza 2, line 2, word 1 is "del."

9. *Quand'io volsi l'altra sera*

Barring begins with one full measure followed by an extended measure. The opening pickup measure given in the edition was determined according to text accents, especially by comparison to mm. 6–8. Residual stanzas are misnumbered, beginning with the second stanza as 1.

10. *Menti, lingua bugiarda*

M. 29, "Seconda parte" above staff.

12. *Chi vuol ch'io m'innamori*

M. 2, B.c., note 3 lacks flat.

16. *Sentirete una canzonetta sopra al bel bocchin*

Second stanza, line 2, word 4 is "nisin."